Born in Nottingham, England, in 1952 into a working class family, William Sharp was educated at Nottingham High School for Boys, and Fitzwilliam College, Cambridge. In 1977, he moved to Norway where he married a young woman from Bergen. They had first met in Hamar a few years earlier and became a couple when she moved to Newcastle for a year to study English. Living first in Bergen and later moving to the Stavanger area where William took up employment in an oil company, he and his wife lived there until retiring and moving to the UK in 2015. He has two daughters and four grandchildren, all living in England.

For K-A, K and A

William Sharp

REVOLVING DOOR

AUSTIN MACAULEY PUBLISHERS™

LONDON • CAMBRIDGE • NEW YORK • SHARJAH

A CIP catalogue record for this title is available from the British Library.

ISBN.9781398497221 (Paperback)
ISBN 9781398497245 (ePub e-book)
ISBN 9781398497238 (Audiobook)

www.austinmacauley.com

First Published 2023
Austin Macauley Publishers Ltd®
1 Canada Square
Canary Wharf
London
E14 5AA

Thank you to all those at Austin Macauley Publishers who have helped to make this book happen and especially to K-A, without whom none of this would have been possible.

Foreword

Suppose you were to write,
telling me that poems are a lie,
a mystery,
apart from all the certainties of life.
And suppose you call it 'Poem'.
For my sake.

Poems I

I look for God

I look for God in cafes and at railway stations
Between the tea cups and the crowds
In unfinished desserts and discarded food wrappings
In half-lived lives and unguarded moments

I am never disappointed

In a woman's glance
A couple's goodbye
A pool of spilled coffee
The Divine rears its head
And catches me unprepared

If God exists
He drinks in cafes
And keeps watch over railway stations
Distributing his comfort with a waitress's smile
Drawing us on with neatly packed parcels of hope
routinely dispensed from strategically placed vending
machines

He must be here

He must be here

How else can such a scene survive?

Why else do people return?

Why else am I catching the waitress's eye and ordering another coffee?

Times

There are times when there is too much time
When the self-sustaining rhythm of the days falters
And the self
Left to itself
Stalls and folds

And there are times
When there is too little time
When the days jostling colliding are swept along on a tide of
activity
And the self
Lost to itself
Lets being be

And then there are those perfect times
When time itself subsides
And the pretty woman in the shampoo commercial
is turning her head once more,
Her hair swinging freely, freely
From north to east to north to west, returning
time and time again
In a perfect sequence of clean slow motion

And anything can happen
And everything can happen
And nothing happens

Mountains

There are those we would be mountains
and sincerely
Not in order to raise them above us
And in doing so set them apart
But simply because they are who they are

You have been a mountain to me

Sustaining me with the generosity of your views
Sheltering me in the nature of your flanks
Restoring me in the shade of your cool valleys
You have loved me as no other would

But both you and I know that there are other purer kinds of
love calling for other kinds of lover

Like the retired urban taxi driver
still ferrying dreamless insomniac passengers through another
long night
Like the amateur poet
baring his soul in well-measured portions to a public hungry
for professional extravagant truths

Like those little rocks in the desert which
having absorbed all day long the intense indifferent heat of
the sun crack open at night along the whole of their length in
a perfectly lonely chorus of echoing whispering sighs

Saints fools and rocks have no need of mountains.

I Have Not Travelled

I have not travelled
My thoughts have not wandered

Although modern modes of transport oblige
and routine flights of the imagination suffice
neither has carried me to the far corners of the earth

Opportunities there were
and invitations many
From arbitrary groups of open free-spirited people
caught up in their curiously homogeneous search for broader
horizons

I chose a different route

Here
At home
I remained

Day after day
Year after year

Forming barely significant repetitive ripples of sound
with carefully predetermined movements of my lips
A desperate band of blind waves sent out on their
necessary
vain
inert journey into space

Believing

If I have to believe
let me believe in timetables

In page upon page of neatly aligned columns and rows
carefully intersecting at strategically chosen times and places
telling me where to be
and when to be there

And which I can consult
at any time
and anywhere

—by the grace of modern technology
with its heavenly host of perfectly placed satellites—

To check in real time
as I step down from the bus
or from the train onto the platform
that I am where I should be
when I should be there

Only when the signal fails do I lose faith

I Refuse to Think the Worst

I refuse to think the worst
Although it's true that you're late
and the night outside is cold and thick
and the news on the radio is all bad
I know in my self that you're safe

There has been no accident
There will be no tragedy
No such theatrical passions could ever upstage our real life
our quiet life
content as we are to be borne and formed
by the gentle persistent rhythm of ordinary days

And yet
even now
somewhere in the future
a young boy is on the move
Scouting an edge of sea and shore
he is searching, searching for two unassuming stones,
there, side by side in the sand,
similarly moulded and mutually shaped,

worn comfortable and smooth by a lasting repetition of
ephemeral tides.

And as he takes the stones in his hand,
perhaps he will weigh them carefully,
perhaps he will admire their form
(Not that it matters,
nothing like that ever really mattered)
before tossing them,
separately and without a care,
into the vast expanse from which they came.

To Those Who Would Be Heard

To poets
Who insist that their poems should be read aloud

To authors
Who, not content with the humming they generate in people's
heads,
Rush off to recite their latest work at public gatherings

To monks
Who mumble themselves to sleep

To those without speech
Who address each other with loud, intricate movements of
their hands

To lovers
Who betray themselves in whispers on the pillow

To all who would be heard

OK
I admit it
I can see the need

On our solitary, common journey then
From silence
Back to silence
Let us agree at least to listen between the lines

Borders

I don't know why or how
you came to be on the inside
while I
for my part
find myself on the outside

I don't think it's a question of choice
It can't be a question of choice
At least, once out, there's no way in

So where do we meet
you and I?
Somewhere in this human landscape
Is there a place where cultural boundaries subside?
Where the poorly mapped contours of consciousness
harbour some gentler form of relief?

If you edge outwards
and I edge inwards
can we gain some common ground?
Within the narrow, endless borders of no man's land?

On the other side of culture.
Beyond personality.

Poetry

Don't expect to find it in the unexpected intimacy of an arbitrary crowd of football fans
Nor in the rhythmical chanting swaying of 60,000 loosely connected individuals
Not even in the sheltering warmth of an evening stadium floodlit against the cold night sky

Neither will you find it in the simplicity of the game itself
Nor in the intricately crafted movements of the players
As they create and break down in turn surprisingly delicate networks of time and space

No

You will find it in the carefully measured flight of the ball
Instinctively weighted and curved into its inevitable predetermined arc of trajectory
Shaping the air and rippling the net
Primitive lines of beauty unerringly formed by ageless physical waves perfectly described in textbooks

So that time, just for a moment, stands still

All's Well That Ends Well

When I am old
And no longer called upon to give speeches
Or express opinions
Or offer advice on matters of any kind

When no one cares any more
To hear what it is that I might have to say
When I no longer care myself

I will sit in a chair
In a dimly lit corner of the room
Or by the window in the sunlight
And I will utter words at random
Until I speak at last that perfect sentence
All my life has eluded me

Apology

I'm sorry.

I was never very good at it, was I,
this living business?
Never really got the hang of it somehow.
There was always something which didn't ring quite true.

I was desperate to remain true.

There was always something missing, wasn't there?
Things never felt really complete.
Never quite all of a piece, as they say.

I know I should have done better.

Looking back,
older not wiser,
I can see now that I was too busy being faithful,
although to what I'm not sure.

I was determined to be faithful.

Which meant,
in the end,
that I never quite managed to feel,
or give the impression,
that I knew what I was doing.
And worse than that, much worse,
I never learned how to pretend.

Let Go

Believe me
I never objected to your beauty
On the contrary
Your beauty has always been a great comfort to me

And I assure you
I never once let your intelligence come between us
The fact is
Your intelligence flatters me

That others consider you attractive is all to my advantage
Your poise
Your social grace
Your generosity
All of this I admire

If I'm leaving you now
If you find me at my desk writing a lover's farewell note
If I'm wishing you all the best as I manage my belongings
onto that other side of the threshold one very last time

It's because of your need to be these things

Self-Realisation

You were in my dreams again last night
Sexual fantasies of course
I daren't begin to tell you all the things we might have done
together

And then
this morning
you were there

And once again
your smile got in the way
your flesh got in the way
you got in the way

And I found myself thinking once more about all those people
who make plans
Who fill their hearts with ambitious elaborate scenarios for
the future
And who when mapping their ideas onto the real world itself
Contrive somehow to make them fit

And I wonder
I just wonder
When it comes down to it
When all is said and done
When they look back on all that was and might have been

Can they have realised what they were thinking?

Statue

It was morning after breakfast
And the coffee cup which had kept me company throughout
the meal remained.
Still, its scene outlived.
Not defiant, what need to defy?
It had its shape
its mass
its place in the physical world.

Which is when the longing rose in me.

To be as a statue.
Still, surveying the scene.
Not dominating, what need to dominate?
Cast in stone
no need to shape
no need to form
no need to be formed
enduring and indifferent.

And I thought
Perhaps
that might be better.

But how then to resist those natural human needs
To raise an eyebrow
To follow something with one's gaze
To form one's lips into a smile?

Because eventually
inevitably
it would happen
and the merest ripple of life within
would strain the stone to breaking
and shatter the form to pieces

And still I thought
Perhaps
that might be better.

One of Those

I am one of those who refuse to take escalators
One of those who stubbornly shun moving airport walkways
for fear of being taken a gate too far
One of those who prefer to get lost along the way rather than
be ferried faultlessly to their destination by the conveniently
confident voice of a satnav

It's not that I'm against progress
It's just that I'm concerned

Concerned that one day
One day soon
Shops will be writing our wishlists
Apps will be mapping our minds
And we'll all find ourselves carrying smartly designed
handheld devices which cleverly predict what it is we're about
to say

And which eventually
eventually
will say it for us

Sunsets

The sun set this evening
As it does most evenings
Caught between lives
Temporarily adrift at some unnamed UK airport
I resolved to match its progress

And although for the most part it moved secretly across its
sky
I fancied for a moment
As the earth heaved backwards and the sun fell away
That we shared some common fate

But fancy it was
And fancy it must have been
After all, sunsets have their own way of doing things

The sun will probably rise again in the morning
As it does most mornings
Don't wake me
I'll catch it later

The Surprising Longevity of a New Forest Pony

Standing stoically in age-old scene of natural beauty
You pay no heed to short-lived tourists like us

Who come here to sample your stillness
Who come here to borrow your calm

Not made from the same stuff as you we can never make them
our own
Returning too soon lest time should overtake us to the every
day busyness of life

Not fully aware our minds are set on other things

And although our lives span far more years than yours
I sense on leaving that you will be here still long after we're
gone

Poems II

Revolving Door

I envy you revolving door
Your movements all accounted for

All day long you see things through
Your every action right on cue
Know when to move
And when to not
You play the game, you know the plot

Placed full firmly on the ground
Confidently getting round
Never doubting
Always sure
You fill your space, you know the score

Some say you're going nowhere fast
Your equanimity's of the past
You take a turn
And show them then
What goes around comes round again

Lately I'm tired of working out
Just what my life revolves about
Spin me a
Centrifugal force
That's all I need to stay the course

I envy you revolving door
You turn when pushed and nothing more

Being

Do not stir
Take your rest
Ignore the morning long progressed

Though desires and duties
Should insist
Don't heed their call, hold back, resist

Don't let waking dreams of seeing
Blind you to this sense of being

Stay with me
Just be with me
In this naked, first reality

Don't let them fool you
Don't let them rule you
With promises of humanity

For all their knowing
For all its crowing
Is only culture, art and poetry

A Man of Passion

I once knew a man of considerable passion
Who paid no heed to fads or fashion

Who rose each day as the clock struck eight
Who was always punctual, never late

Who very rarely stepped out of line
Who never received a speeding fine

Who had one wife, one home, one car
Who never travelled very far

Who lived quite unexceptionally
Who never once strayed sexually

Who preferred silence to music of any kind
Whose aim in life was a quiet mind

Who to others seemed a boring fellow
So sedate, so mild, so mellow

Who lived in silent desperation
In calm, intense anticipation
Of the day his doings would all be done
Peace attained, the course full run

Who died at the close with little to do
The business of living all seen through

So you see, in his way and after a fashion
He indeed was a man of considerable passion

Another Place

I'd heard talk of art in its rightful place
Deployed along an edge of time and space
Of those who bore witness to consciousness grown
Of seeds of longing in urban hearts sown

So I let my yearning draw me out to the beach
Where art was in sight
And art was in reach
To find only casts of the human race
Rusting time
Consuming space

Who to me said nothing

And I know I'm to blame
Mine is the lacking
Mine is the shame
For artists and experts and laymen and all
Say these level-headed men to humanity call
And if that's the truth, and if that's the case
I'd left my humanity another place

Sitting by the Window

You're sitting by the window
Looking out at life beyond
Thinking perhaps of days to come
And of other days soon gone

And maybe you're withdrawing
When perhaps you ought to stay
But the evening light is calling
At the closing of the day

I'm sitting by the window
When a man comes into view
And there's something in his presence
Which makes me think of you

Perhaps it's his keen interest
In the living and in change
Or the little imperfections
He would like to rearrange

And maybe I'm recalling
When perhaps I should renew
But the future keeps on stalling
And the present missed its cue

So let's sit beside the window
For another while or so
We'll just wait here by the window
Until it's time to go

Some Say Love

Some say love's nothing more than illusion
Born of chemo-hormonal confusion
I look at you and you look at me
And both see the person we want to see

And perhaps it's true, at least of the fall
But of long-standing love it says little at all
The elemental source of that bond lies may be
Far beyond this burning in you and in me

For this love, say, within us which first appeared
One fine, rare day when you and I grew near
Neither falters nor fades when we're apart
No chemistry then to fire its heart

No—our love is constant, independent and free
Ever enduring when neither you nor I see
It's the singular outcome of our repeated troth
Enjoining, encompassing and enriching us both

The World Did Not Stop Turning

The world did not stop turning as you drew your final breath
Nor did the rhythm of the living falter at your death

But that I in my aloneness should yet still want to live
That is the cardinal sinning I never can forgive

Gone my life's companion, lost my faithful wife
The only thing remaining this faithless hold on life

It's nothing I have chosen, it's nothing I regret
Not born of any gratitude nor to settle any debt

For though in heaven no place awaits me and in God I have
no stake
The choice to live or else to die was never mine to make.

A Few Verses

The Universe

The universe, some say, will grow
For a few more billion years or so
And then, at last, begin to shrink
Which makes one stop, and start to think
Will things return to where things began,
Resulting in a new Big Bang?
Does time itself then ebb and flow.
Do all our histories come and go?
And is this our third, fifth, tenth time round,
And are those people quite profound
Who speak to us of previous lives,
Whose travelling thought routinely dives
Into the past and future too,
Which the present constantly passes through?

How many the times
And whatever the score,
I've probably written this poem before!

The Writing on the Wall

A wall as a wall is no wall at all
If with art it is made something more of
For while a wall as a wall is respected by all
Art one can never be sure of

Furthermore:

A work of art is an acquisition
Used to fill an awkward space
While a poem's modest ambition
Is to steal art's pride of place

So take my advice:

Hold onto your self and keep your walls clear
Hold onto your pride and your space
Leave the cultural elite to jive and compete
About the virtue of a spiritual race

Let them clutter their walls
Let them fill up their space
Let them trade acquisitions and own pride of place

For of one thing I'm certain
Of one thing I'm sure
It must be true now
If it wasn't before:
'Though the writing on the wall points its finger at us all
Relax, take it easy
It's probably just graffiti!

Me and You and We Two

Sustaining one's identity
Can be a tiresome thing to do
You have to keep on doing the things
Which confirm that you are you

But should you toe a different line
In a brave attempt to redefine
In trying to change just who you are
You'll find you won't get very far

Change your ways, change your style
Become another for a while
Tired of trying things off the shelf
You'll soon revert to a truer self

And in truth it may not matter much
Whether you be I or I be you
For imagine if we were to swap
Who'd get the better of the two?

Self-Searching

I fashioned me a costume, some currency and kit
'Though to my way of thinking they didn't quite fit
But after a while
I grew into their style
And resolved to make the best of it

All things considered things suited me fine
I could sense what was theirs, others knew what was mine
And truth to tell
I functioned quite well
Feeling pretty substantial most of the time

But lately I'm feeling some kind of resistance
A sense of detachment, an awareness of distance
I'm missing cohesion, I'm wanting coherence
What once seemed real is now just appearance

I can ride this thing out, of that I feel sure
I know what's needed, I'm onto the cure
I'm staying clean
I'm in a routine
I'll regain what it was that sustained me before

The person I became those years ago
Was perhaps not me, it's hard to know
But you have to be someone
If only to get on
And one's good as the other as far as things go

Efficiency

Efficiency as a value holds little virtue
For non-believers who prefer to
See growth and profit and progress deferred to
Values a sight more true

Time is money and money is time
A slogan amorally so sublime
That to challenge its truth is deemed a crime
Some new age con man's paradigm

For just whose morals can compel?
What we ought – who can tell?
The goal be heaven, the goal be hell
Our charge is to do things well

When there is no why, only how
When there is no then, only now
Perspective reason should endow
Emotions disavow

When ethics to aesthetics pale
When moral compass points to no avail
Efficiency's the value which will prevail
When all other values fail

Afterword

Should these leaves after me fall as they
Broken, free on autumn day

Framed against impartial sky
Beheld the moment by passers-by

Arousing attention the briefest while
Raising an eyebrow lifting a smile

Sharing a singular point of view
Of mutual seasons soon passed through

Then falling to ground to decay and to rot
Taking refuge in common lot

May those passing witnesses judge with care
The sentence or two which touched them there

And should none pass by and no-one see
Still there's untold comfort in poetry

Notes

Another Place

Written as a response to Anthony Gormley's art installation entitled 'Another Place' when it was exhibited on Sola beach near Stavanger, Norway. Arranged as a human group walking out into the sea, the various figures, all in the form of a cast of Gormley himself, stretched from the edge of the airport, across the beach and into the sea itself. There was quite a lot written in the local newspapers at the time, mostly positive. People were even inspired to write and send in poems. Again, overwhelmingly positive. I've never been a great fan of art out in the open. I find it all just a bit too pretentious. Especially when works of art on this scale simply arouse people's curiosity and end up functioning as a kind of happening based on consumerism. Which was how I experienced 'Another Place'. So I ended up writing – not altogether intentionally – a pretentious and somewhat irreverent poem about the artwork and the attention it received. The irony of the poem, some of it obvious, some of it less so (for example, as far as I can recall, it was important that the heads of the many figures should all be at the same height) is moderated by the concession admitted in the closing line which may be seen as acknowledging the artist's good intention. If the point of art is to elicit a reaction from the public then 'Another Place' exhibited on Sola beach was a resounding success!

Sitting by the window

In memory of Magnus Jensen 1920–2002. Although written with my late father-in-law in mind, this poem can hopefully be appreciated by anyone who has experienced loss.

Some say love

Written while in search of an appropriate poem to recite at my younger daughter's wedding. Everything we came across seemed to be too romantic or too serious or too sentimental. Both bride and groom had university degrees in subjects related to biochemistry, so the idea was to express the theme of love playfully but sincerely with a measured amount of sentiment, drawing on biochemical imagery. The reader may have problems getting the line '*The elemental source of that bond lies may be*' to fit the rhythm of the poem. Try putting emphasis on '*that*' and read '*may be*' as written i.e. as two separate words!